I0139629

Forbidden Dancer

a Collection of Poems

JORDAN DEAN

All rights reserved.

No part of this publication may be translated, reproduced, or transmitted in any form or by any means, in whole or in part, electronic or mechanical including photocopying, recording, or by any information storage or retrieval system without prior permission in writing from the author.

The views expressed in this work are solely those of the author and do not necessarily reflect the views of the publisher, and the publisher hereby disclaims any responsibility for them.

Text copyright © Jordan Dean

Cover Photograph copyright © Kellyanne Limbiye

First Edition: December, 2017

The moral right of the author has been asserted.

Published by JDT Publications
Port Moresby, National Capital District, Papua New Guinea
Email: jdtpublications@gmail.com

National Library of Papua New Guinea
Cataloguing-in-Publication entry:

Dean, Jordan. 1984 — .
    Forbidden Dancer: A Collection of Poems.

ISBN-13: 978-9980-89-985-9

1. Poetry, Papua New Guinea. 1. Collection of Poems
PNG/821-dc 22

Printed in USA by CreateSpace Independent Publishing.

To my family and readers with love.

May this poetry collection inspire, edify, enlighten, and challenge us to explore ourselves, the world around us and even the unseen.

JORDAN DEAN

CONTENTS

JORDAN DEAN

Culture & Modernity

FORBIDDEN DANCER

I am the forbidden dancer
The poet who can save this world
With the melody of the ocean.

A dancer of silent whispers
Chanting ballads to the pearl
Scattering sacred poetry
Across the horizon.

A dancer impersonating the dove
Reciting spells from my ancestors
Scented with frangipani blossoms.

A dancer carving the new moon
Blooming hearts of young lovers
Revitalizing the soul of the dance.

A dancer painting the stars
And seasons of yam harvest
In my rhythmic movements.

A dancer of timeless silence
Within the shadows of dawn
Awakening the spirits of my ancestors
The forbidden dance is the ritual of life.

CHANTS OF THE SPIRITS

When rains didn't come
I placed a coconut shell
And asked the spirits
To send rain.

Before a fishing trip
I chewed ginger
And asked the spirits
For plenty of tuna.

Like my ancestors
I danced the *daiyo*[1]
And burnt herbs
To protect my spirit.

I chanted to the spirits
With deep thoughts
Diluted by
Western education.

---

[1] Daiyo: Traditional dance

BWEBWESO KUYOKUYO

Bwebweso kuyokuyo
Kuyokuyo'yogu
dedeligu ededela
Sine kubukubuto
A sine kalamalai
Yasiyale yolemuya
Kuyoyo kuyoyo dedeligu
Idedela tainigu.

BWEBWESO FLOWER

Bwebweso flower
Mersmerise me
Make me shiver
Girl of the shore
With a strong heart
That loves me
Come to me
Shiver for me
Come to me
Tremble for me.

BUYUWA IYAUMANI

Buyuwa iyaumani
Yayaumani buibui
Iyaumani weki weki
Yayaumani weki weki
Mwagugu woiyawa
Maninigu kokom
Welabana kedaloa
Sanapu kedakubwa.

LIKE THE OCTOPUS

Like the octopus
That changes colours
To disguise itself
I change colours too.

Like the octopus
With a large head
And demonic face
Spirits flee from my path.

TAPIOCA DANCE

Swaying under the moonlight
Rhythmical in our pursuit
Her legs touched the sky
Toes tapping on the moon
Flowers flourish and bloom
I tipped the moon over
Ecstasy abounds, we convulse
The moon spins, darkness shines
In a blink my star is engulfed
I now dance within her moon
Wave upon wave
Rippling through her
In a crescendo
Passion explodes
Her moon trembles
A gush of milk and honey
Tapioca dance continues.

AMBAI

(Published in Crocodile Prize Anthology - 2016)

Cold morning dew
From the misty Daulo pass
Kissed her strong feet
The raggianas' sang their songs
Of love when she was near.

Sun rises to brighten her day
Orchids bowed their heads
Spellbound by her beauty
Her ancestors' spirits smile
Lost in a moment of tranquility
As she silently walks by.

She leaves a wake of calmness
That puts fierce warriors at ease
She wears the feathers
Of the bird of paradise
As a crown.

Ambai²
Daughter of nature
Her spirit is so free
I've never seen such beauty
But she never noticed me.

---

² Ambai: Young lady or girl

7

THE DANCER

In all the glory and splendor
Of her traditional *bilas*[3]
And her painted body
Like a beautiful rainbow
She swayed to the rhythm of the wind
Fingers pluck across the setting sun
Tracing the legends of her ancestors
On foams of ocean rippling.

From the womb of dawn
She danced to the melodies of the *sagali*[4]
At the first sound of her smooth voice
Her ancestors' spirits are stirred
And my poor heart is crippled
By her heavenly beauty.

---

[3] Bilas: Dressing or costume
[4] Sagali: Traditional drum or traditional feast and celebration

PACIFIC GODDESS
(Published in Spill Words)

Weary, dying sun
Smiled, kissing the calm ocean
Adorned crested waves.

Girl with golden hair
Watches the sunset retreat
Into liquid gold.

Girl from the islands
Her eyes like sparkling sapphire
Her voice like spring rain.

Her lips like velvet
Her hands like a soothing river
Her smile like sunshine.

She is a goddess
Torturing me with her eyes
My Pacific Aphrodite.

GIRL WITH A BAGI
(Published in Spill Words)

Girl with a *bagi*[5]
I am mesmerized by your beauty
You shine brightly like the midnight sun
Your reflection is like the moon shadows.

Your figure sparkles like the Eastern star
You walk elegantly like a pacific princess
Your hair is curly like the ocean waves.

Around your neck
Is a pearl necklace
From our native home
Where the sun rises.

Daughter of the ocean
And the choice of my parents
I worship you silently with my eyes.

---

[5] Bagi: Shell necklace

BLACK PEARL

Black pearl
Plucked from the atolls
Of my homeland
Your untamed eyes
Burn with tenderness
Lips so red
And rosy cheeks
Your smile carves
Out the ocean
Lightning flashes
When you talk.

Too many stars
Too many pebbles
Only one black pearl
Come grow old with me
Your ebony skin
Is sun-kissed
Sparkles in my eye
The joy in my heart
Take me beyond
The moon and stars.

PURPLE DOVE

Graceful *bunebune*[6]
On dancing wings
Searching for a home
Away from this cold place
Where daydreams are silent
And midnight sun never shines
Chasing rainbows in the dark
Another day to her destiny
Sunsets in endless grey.

Delicate wings carry her
Into the velvet, setting sun
Bunebune lies in twilight sleep
Dreaming purple colour deep
Midnight sun will shine again
Be strong my love
Sacred purple dove!

---

[6] Bunebune: Dove

Tattooed Face

Behind my tattooed face
Is a face full of love and grace
Beneath these intricate tattoo
Is a glowing heart
That welcomes strangers
To those rocky cliffs I loved the most
Or to grainy softness of white beaches
And as green evening wafts the spray
Through slender coconut palms swaying away
You just might glimpse at my feathery shadow
And fear that I eat humans raw.

PLASTIC BEAUTY

Gone is the steel wool hair
Now relaxed and gleaming
With the use of Africa's Best
Sometimes permed or dyed
To a golden-brown, blonde lass.

Once your lips were *buai*[7] red
Now covered with lipsticks
Gone is the frangipani fragrance
Now you use a lot of perfumes
Meri[8] or chemist?

Before your hands were strong
Now delicate and hardly cooks
Your chocolate skin is smooth
Thanks to the lotions and creams
With your pencil-thin eye brows
You crucify me with your smile.

Before I could pay you
With [9]*bagi* and [10]*mwali*
Now I'll sweat my guts
Until my ebony butt is sore
To pay fifty thousand kina
For your plastic beauty.

---

[7] Buai: Betel nut
[8] Meri: Girl or lady
[9] Bagi: Shell necklace
[10] Mwali: Arm shell

NO MORE TAPA

No more tapa
Now we have jeans and six pockets
Bagi[11] and *mwali*[12] are things of the past
Now we pay our women with money
A road will be constructed here
To bring rice and tinned fish to us
We don't need yams and taro.

No more *sagali*[13]
Now we have Sony Hi-Fi radios
Bob Marley singing he shot the sheriff
But our Waigani sheriffs are alive
And riding flashy vehicles
We cut down our trees, saw the logs
Build nightclubs for the party freaks
To legitimize adultery and AIDS.

No more *bwabwale*[14]
Now we pretend to be sorry with a few tears
We don't respect our dead relatives anymore
All we worry about is money and beer
Once the *moni-man*[15] build new mines
We only chew our *buai*[16] and gossip
Where is our royalties?

---

[11] Bagi: Shell necklace
[12] Mwali: Arm shell
[13] Sagali: Traditional drum or traditional feast and celebration
[14] Bwabwale: Feast in memory of the dead
[15] Moni-man: Rich men
[16] Buai: Betel nut

IDENTITY

I tried to claim
A Latin accent
Hollywood looks
Scandinavian eyes
And a French appetite
I spoke fancy English
Wore an American Nike shoe
Dressed like an Aussie
And drove a Ford Ranger.

I was Akon or Chris Brown
Eminem, Usher, Shane Ward
Even a Justin Timberlake
But to my disgrace
I was stripped bare
And realised that I had
Papua New Guinean blood
Melanesian bones
And Pacific dreams.

CHILDREN OF FERGUSSON

We are the children of the ocean
Sun and moon are our parents
Born with chocolate colored skin
We toiled the blessed earth
And feasted during the *sagali*[17]
We sailed the ocean in our *sailao*[18]
To distant lands on the Kula Trade
We climbed *Oya Tabu*[19] to reach the stars
And danced the sacred *daiyo*[20]
With the spirits of *Bwebweso*[21]
We are strong and bold
Gifted and talented
Intelligent enough to lead
We are the children of Fergusson.

---

[17] Sagali: Traditional drum or traditional feast and celebration
[18] Sailau: Sailing canoe
[19] Oya Tabu: Sacred mountain
[20] Daiyo: Traditional dance
[21] Bwebweso: Place of the dead

WELABANA

Welabana[22] dancing
Under the dim moonlight
Twirling without a face
Fireflies dance with her
She sings to herself
As the moon illuminates
Her silhouettes.

Dawn approaches
In tranquil shadow
She fades away
Into its embrace.

---

[22] Welabana: Witch or sorcerer

BASTARD CHILD

I was born last night
During the *karim leg*[23]
I stared at the grey mist
The first breath of dawn
Mother named me Boko
After my legendary ancestor
I was there without a father
Or whoever exactly.

I was born last night
Among many feasts
Spread in thin air
When I asked mother
About my father
She just shook her head
And said to me
'You're the reflection
Of reality and truth
Be strong my son!'

---

[23] Karim leg: Courting ceremony

SINS OF OUR FATHERS
(Published on PNG Attitude)

Our fathers ate the fruit
From the forbidden tree
Inside the *Haus Tambaran*[24]
Their wives were witches
Who married for fortune.

Our fathers slept around
With those two kina ladies
For a few nights pleasure
Now our purse is empty.

Now our fathers are dead
Our sons have no land
Our daughters sleep with
Old white and yellow men.

Our provoked sisters
Diluted with western ideology
Keep yapping like dogs
That Adam and Eve were equal
But wasn't it through Eve
That *sangumas*[25] haunt us?

Now our fathers' spirits
Grieve from the graves
At the misery of their sins.

---

[24] Haus Tambaran: Parliament House
[25] Sanguma: Bad spirits or demons

OLOTO

Fergusson Island man
His skin is strong
Like a bush *magani*[26]
His eyes are brown
Like the coconut palms
His hair is soft and curly
Like the ocean waves
But when he smiled
His teeth were black
Like the seeds of
A ripe watermelon.

That one how?
You know it already
That one, *buai*[27] teeth.

That one who?
That one, our brother
His name is *Oloto*[28].

---

[26] Magani: Wallaby
[27] Buai: Betel nut
[28] Oloto: Man

RISPETTO: BLACK BEAUTY
(Published on PNG Attitude)

Fifty years ago, I walked my land naked
Flaunted my black booty with grace
Dimdims[29] said my customs were crooked
Said my naked black butt was a disgrace
Now on Runways, my beauty is on display
I'm confused with their dishonorable ways
I'm asked to wear skimpy pants and bikini
Not the future I envisioned for my *pikinini*[30]!

---

[29] Dimdim: Expatriate or white man
[30] Pikinini: Child or children

RISPETTO: T'SAK VALLEY

Twelve hour bus ride all night long
Home is a thousand miles up the highway
Up in the mountains where I belong
Mumu[31] pork and *kaukau*[32] of yesterday
Cold, frosty sunrise in Mt. Hagen
My journey to T'sak Valley began
I dance in the Sugar Loaf mist and rain
T'sak Valley blood runs in my vein.

---

[31] Mumu: Traditional highlands style of cooking
[32] Kaukau: Sweet potato

SONNET: MY ANCESTORS
(Published in Creative Talents Unleashed)

Long ago, my ancestors roamed this place
These mountains, jungles and mighty rivers
With bow and arrows and mud on their face
They were cannibals that fed on livers.

From open savannahs to coastal plain
Rich with a vast range of animal life
They could make storm clouds and bring rain
My ancestors lived free and without strife.

Missionaries came and said they're unholy
You should never judge their tattooed cover
Why say their black magic was ungodly
When your fabled Jesus walked on water?

Never look at my people with distaste
And never draw such conclusions in haste.

Sonnet: Returning Home

Pearl of the ocean, Fergusson Island
Though I may roam the streets of Port Moresby
I will return to my humble homeland
Reminisce all my childhood days gone by.

Beyond the rainbow and beyond the skies
A road descends, golden trail of the past
The blue horizon flashes before my eyes
Homeward bound, relish childhood dreams at last.

I return to the place that knows my name
A place of comfort, free from all the pain
My eyes sparkle brighter than a flame
There is warmth and sunshine after the rain.

I pray that we will prosper one day
If we let the Almighty lead the way.

JORDAN DEAN

SONNET: PAPUA NEW GUINEA
(Published in Dissident Voice Magazine)

In the Pacific lies a land of gold
An island floating on a sea of oil
She is my home and there I shall grow old
On these open plains and earth I shall toil.

Whether you are watching her ocean waves
Enjoying the stars and moonlight night sky
Or exploring all of her wondrous caves
She keeps calling me in a haunting cry.

Early sunrise brings hope for another day
Another day of praying for the best
Her sunsets give a magical display
Putting troubled minds and children to rest.

She has embroiled me so tight with her heart
Her mighty grip, I can't fight nor depart.

MOUNTAIN ORCHESTRA
(Published on PNG Attitude)

From the top and steady now
Looking up while falling down
On these mountains, we dance
Dramatize our fall from grace.

Cold misty mountain range
Climb them all to reach the stage
Where our love notes sound so sweet
Where the cicadas sing as we sleep.

Bring the fire dancers, bring the tears
Everything we lost over the years
Start the thunder, beat the drums
All we know we must become.

Heartstrings won't make us see
How they slayed our destiny
GDP forecasts can't change our past
Shooting stars that fell too fast.

Feel the *garamut*[33] shake the ground
All the truth was never found
Hear the sea gull as it cries
Every tear for every lie.

Graceful dove sing your song
Tell me where I went wrong
Dim the stage lights to a glow
Just enough to watch her go.

---

[33] Garamut: Drum

Looking back to see my birthplace
Asking why there's no warm embrace
Counting stars to find the mean
You and me was just a dream.

ONCE UPON A TIME (MAMA)

Once upon a time
Mama had big and firm breasts
A lusty Australian sucked all the milk
Now her weak breasts hang empty
Our minerals gone!

Once upon a time
Mama had bushy pubic hair
A horny Asian shaved it smooth
Now she is hairless and bare
Our forests gone!

Once upon a time
Mama wore a grass skirt
Now she is stripped naked
Exploited and raped
Our money gone!

Once upon a time
Her sons, future chiefs
Were warriors with strong penis
Now just gays and pole dancing
Screwed doggy style for a million kina
Our future gone!

Cry, my people
Mama is no more
We are no more!

PROSTITUTE

Your twenty year old
Seductiveness
Torment my thoughts
What a pity for me.

I asked you out for lunch
You called me a loser
And that I don't meet
Your high standards
What a pity for me.

But on fortnight Friday
A grey-haired executive
Picked you up in his Prado
What a low life bitch!
I feel sorry for you.

PRETTY VAVINE

She loves to party, have a good time
She looks so hearty, feeling fine
She loves to smoke Dunhill cigarette.

She dresses up in designer clothes
She is the scramble
And she moves with passion.

She belongs to the nightclub
The dance floor —
Attached to the white can
Cigarette after cigarette
Smoking and laughing.

She enjoys the weekend most
In tight jeans and mini top
She goes off to party
At the Gold Club or Shooters
She is every man's pretty *vavine*[34].

---

[34] Vavine: Young lady

COMMODITY

Your home is a sight to behold
It shines with a thousand lights
You dress like a super model every day
But you married for wealth, not for love
Though you live in a grand palace
You're only a dove in a filthy cage
Neighbours think you're happy
You're not, though you seem to be
It's sad when I think of your wasted life
For youth cannot mate with age
And your beauty was sold
For an old man's gold.

MOTHERLAND

Guided by the sunrise
I navigated the world in my *sailau*[35]
Searching for happiness
But was never satisfied.

I came to the end of daylight
And faced the womb of darkness
But when I touched my face
I realized there were tears
And my spirit was cold
All that I thought I loved
And needed was gone
I was stripped naked
Shivering in my misery.

At noon I sailed towards the sunset
And came across a deserted island
The embers of their fire
Still glowing in the darkness.

I looked down, looked deep
And saw my begotten umbilical cord
Beneath the ashes
A voice from deep within
Drew me closer until I reached out
And put my fingers on my blessed cord
I had come home at last.

Slowly, meticulously
I rekindled the embers
And burnt away my dead body
When it was gone
I was no longer naked.

---

[35] Sailau: Saling canoe

My Name is Boko
(Published on PNG Attitude)

My name is Boko
Son of the Earth
Great grandson of Nabwalega
Born under a village hut
Using herbs from the forest
In the ways of my ancestors.

Rain drummed against the earth
And the wind whispered welcome
Nature embraced me warmly
Trapped between heaven and hell
Meandering through the jungle
I followed my ancestors' spirits
Spells and chants were imparted
Waded through the twilight grove
And drank from the spirits well
I ate fruits of knowledge
Each fruit sweeter
Than the one before
I gathered the pearls
On Digalagala Island
Filled my mind with its wisdom
To save my people's ailments.

Recalling my ancestors words
I returned to my birth place
My people no respect
For our land and sea
I wept, the pain
Reverberating in my heart
While my soul floated
Above the ocean
The earth beneath
My feet trembled

FORBIDDEN DANCER

Thunder roared
And lightning clashed
The spirits were not happy.

I summoned the spirits
To relieve the maladies
And make the yams grow
I stopped the rain
And calmed the storm
I invoked healing
Supernatural powers.

My name is Boko
Son of the Earth
Great grandson of Nabwalega
In the spirits voice I call
I am the envoy
To link two worlds.

SILENT THOUGHTS

1.
An empty street
An empty home
An empty room
A silent moon.

I am here on the balcony
Sipping a glass of Jack Daniels
Silent thoughts at two am
Drift through my mind
Just me and my thoughts
Alone.

2.
Father once asked me
Have you ever climbed Everest?
Have you ever sailed the ocean?
Have you ever touched the rainbow?

Reach for the moon
Even if you miss it
You'll still have the stars.

Listen to your heartbeat
It only takes one step
To start a journey
Of a thousand miles.

3.
A wise man also said
Just keep walking in that direction
To the end of the tunnel
The wind will blow in your face
But keep walking.

Hear that voice inside you
It's the call of your heart
Follow it and you will find
The passage out of the dark.

4.

A thousand silent thoughts
Bottled up inside my head
Wish I could turn back time
Freeze all those happy moments
One last time.

5.

Daydreams are silent
Midnight sun will never shine
The *hiri*[36] will carry you to paradise
Just the ramblings of a fool
Who pretends to be a poet.

I was halfway to the moon
When I slipped and fell
To the bottom of the ocean
In darkness there lies hope.

It doesn't matter
Where you come from
Or where you've been
All that matters
Is where you're going.

6.

Midnight whispers
Lovers giggle and cuddle up
Copulating —
Will this country's health care

---

[36] Hiri: Monsoon winds

And education system
Cater for the population boom?
7.
Somewhere in the distance
Impoverished children
Gape with empty eyes
While rich old men
Spoil their young dates
To a fancy buffet.

Men are born equal
But some live in palaces
And others live in squatters.

8.
It's too cold outside
For angels to fly
I keep my hopes and dreams
Inside of me
No one sees the bruises
That I'm covering
An angel dies.

I'm just a simple guy
I don't drink latte or cappuccino
And I don't eat lasagna every day.

I love my highlands *mumu*[37]
And my highlands *kumu*[38]

9.
Memories that were locked away
Somewhere in the deepest corners
Of my mind emerge

---

[37] Mumu: Traditional highlands style of cooking
[38] Kumu: Vegetables

Thought the feeling would go away.

But your voice and face
Keep appearing in my mind
Your beautiful eyes
Did your parents steal
The stars from the sky
And put them in your eyes?

My head says yes
But my heart says no
Wish I never had to choose
I've been walking down
This same old road.

Maybe one day
Our paths will cross
Somewhere on the horizon.

10.
But everywhere I turn
I see reflections of all the lies
Life is a big illusion.

Silent thoughts wander
Around in my mind
Like a jigsaw puzzle
On this cold, lonely morning.

I wish my mind would stop thinking
And maybe I'll find some peace.

Love & Emotions

SIMPLE PLEASURES

I love ordinary things
Beautiful things
Mirrored by the sun and moon
  a little coffee
  a little sunlight
  a little music
  a little poetry
Midnight musings
Under velvet skies
I drink from the moons rays
And listen to the silence
  a little faith
  a little hope
  a little love
Makes this world beautiful
Simple pleasures of life.

FOOT PRINTS

Somewhere in the sands of time
I found your footprints
Fragile memories of yesterday
  a fleeting smile
  a whispered promise
  a pledge everlasting
  a passion once penned
On tear-stained pages
Words left unspoken
And set adrift on the ocean.

The harshness of reality
Waves efface your footprints
A love once written
Upon these sand
Now an empty space.

ANGEL

Straightened hair? Check
Make up? Check
High heels? Check
Sexy Lady? Double check
She looks in the mirror
'Who are you?'
She asks her reflection
Perfection personified.

She walks with such grace,
All marvel at her lovely face
She is an angel
My heart aches
Love is blind
And so am I.

FORBIDDEN LOVER

Beyond the echoing darkness
A soft voice whispered to my ear
Beckoning from the deep shadows
And cold fingers touched my cheeks
Struggling with mixed emotions
I couldn't see who it was
But as darkness turned to light
As the cold fingers turned warm
And the haunting mask removed
I realized it was you
My forbidden lover.

SOLITUDE

On this cold February evening
I gaze out across the ocean
The horizon is empty
Only a single star shines in the sky
Casting shadows on my soul.

Are there butterflies where you walk?
Are you watching the stars
That glitter above the water
Like strings of sparkling diamonds?
Or just listening to the tide moaning
Softly on the shore?
Is the ocean calm?

On this lonely shore
Where we pledged our love
And wrote our promises in the sand
I'll sit and wait for eternity
Until the water forgets to sparkle again.

LOVE BITE

Lingering like a tattoo
On my neck
Very red and sore but
Envied by unlucky folks
Because this tattoo
Is a souvenir from
The sacred moments in
Eden.

POETRY

Passionate
Outpouring of my
Emotions revealed
Through
Real life experiences
Yoked with tears.

MY DREAM GIRL

(Published in the UniTarvur, University of Papua New Guinea, 2003)

Out of a misty dream, she emerged
A sweet and angelic beauty
Wearing the melancholy sunset
In her hair.

She carried the looks of the rainbow
And her frangipani smile shook me to the core
So cute that I couldn't help but stare
Her voice was like the nightingale
Welcoming the first light of a new day
And her touch was so intimate
It was like haven.

Into her lovely arms she took me
And flew away to that long lost paradise;
Where the rivers flowed with milk and honey
And the roses were always in full blossom.

Our eyes met for a second
And I realized I had been beaten once again
By this heavenly, young lady
Hell bent on wrecking my sleep.

LOVE IS A ROSE

Love is a single, scarlet rose
It brings momentary beauty with its blossom
The dampness of its petals from dewdrops
Are like tears and heart sheds.
Love is a rose which you treasure
Until you're hurt by its thorns
The rose will die and wither
The memories will remain
But the plant will flower again and again.

RECREATIONAL LEAVE

If I ever fall in love again
The love I so freely give
Will be full of passion
And run deep as the ocean.

My heart has been shattered
More than I care to recall
Piece by piece I gathered
Pieces that were scattered
Placed them where they belong
Cracks and scars remain
Though unseen.

For now my heart
Has left an official memo
Saying it's out of the office
And on recreational leave.

UNSPOKEN WORDS

I asked you last night
To tell me something
Before you fell asleep.

So many things on your mind
Not a single word did you utter
You'd rather sing a melody
Open up like a budding flower
When you're lying in my arms
Feeling my breath against you.

I promise to turn hell into heaven
A wilted flower into a blooming rose
If only you'd let me be the wings
That keeps your heart in the clouds.

For now, let's be mute
Listen to the deafening silence
For your words will remain
Unspoken.

COFFEE

Not too hot
Not too cold
Just perfect enough
To warm my heart.

Sipped it slow
To enjoy the
Conversational aroma
And cinnamon sarcasm.

The cups were left
Half-filled
It wasn't
About the coffee.

MASK

Do you see me?
Do you really see through me?
Then can you tell me who I am?
Cause if you asked me
I don't know where I stand
I smiled at you
And your heart flipped
At the different shades of grey
I use as a mask
Cause I myself can see
Behind the mask of whom
I want to be.

Yesterday Once More

I remember yesterday
You left with a handshake
Tears and parting words
After all these years
All I feel is a shadow
Of an afterglow of you.

A starless night
Chasing dreams I can't touch
If only I could visit
Yesterday once more.

Tonight I walk this path
Remembering when the sky
Was beautiful.

DESOLATION

(Published in Dissident Voice Magazine)

And once again
I'm left shivering
In the cold.

The moon doesn't shine
Shooting stars have disappeared
In the ocean of fallen hearts
I try not to drown.

Desolation is only a word
Whispered
How can you not fall
In love with emptiness?
For in the solitude
I've found my way home
Loneliness is beautiful.

OH POETESS!

Oh poetess!
Let your heart be my abode.

If it's frozen like ice
I'll warm it up with
The glow of my love and care.

If it is deep like the ocean
I'll transform myself
Into a pearl to live there.

If it is barren
I'll plough and sow
Seeds of passion and mirth.

And if it is like a cave
Dark and mysterious
I'll enter as a ray of light.

Oh poetess!
Let me abide in your heart.

PACIFIC GODDESS
(Published in Spill Words)

Weary, dying sun
Smiled, kissing the calm ocean
Adorned crested waves.

Girl with golden hair
Watches the sunset retreat
Into liquid gold.

Girl from the islands
Her eyes like sparkling sapphire
Her voice like spring rain.

Her lips like velvet
Her hands like a soothing river
Her smile like sunshine.

She is a goddess
Torturing me with her eyes
Beautiful Aphrodite.

MY MOONSHINE

My dear moonshine
Kiss me faithfully
Within your graceful light.

My dear universe
Cradle me in your bosom
Of a million gentle stars.

My dear sunshine
Save me from darkness
With your beckoning warmth.

My dear lady
Captivate my heart
And mesmerize my soul.

ESCAPING THE SEA

Wave after wave
Her possessiveness
Washed over me
Her jealous tide
Carried me out to open seas
I'm hanging on for dear life
I had given up hope
And was sinking fast
Drowning under
Dominating waves
I drifted around
And came within shore
More nagging waves
Crashed over me
Trying to pull me
Back to the raging sea
I swam to the shore
Now the sea is calm
Tempting me to go back
Feeling solid ground
I escape from the sea.

Broken Butterfly

One day I embraced
A broken butterfly
With both of my hands
I surrounded it
With a cocoon of love
To heal its delicate wings
Until it could fly again
My beautiful butterfly.

Dreams

The sparkle in your eyes
Is where I yearn to dance
A pirouette of colors upon your soul
Watch me as I twist and turn
Breathe in my prisms, feel the burn
Remember, my pondering poet
Imagination is what we create
But our dreams are worth
All the effort that it takes.

SHE IS NOT A ROSE

She is not a rose
You can't pluck her
Only to watch her wither.

She is not a cup of latte
You can't sweeten her up
Only to suit your appetite.

She is not a rainbow
You can't delight in her colours
Only when she's appealing.

She is not a cockatoo
You can't dismiss her voice
When you're weary of her.

She is a woman
Strong, worthy, insightful
She needs no comparison
To validate her worth.

SONNET: MASKED LADY

Hidden behind her cold and hateful mask
Is a lady pretending to be strong
Someone to love and care is all she ask
I tried to unmask her but I was wrong.

Hidden behind her pretty smiling face
Is a lady that is barely breathing
Broken up inside with no warm embrace
And a crippled heart that is still bleeding.

Hidden behind her sweet, angelic eyes
Are the tears she cried in the falling rain
In the dark, truth held together with lies
She gave her heart but it was all in vain.

I'm hoping for her eyes to turn my way
If only I knew the right words to say.

SONNET: CHILDHOOD DREAMS

In the heart of the squatter settlements
A son of a poor man was born with dreams
While big men boast about developments
Carefully hiding all their dirty schemes.

Free health care and basic education
No shoes or bag, he went to public school
Learnt English and bits of calculations
Well-to-do kids thought he was just a fool.

He graduated with flying colors
Through all the struggles and toil, he stood tall
And went on to become a great doctor
Achieving his childhood dream to heal all.

Kings rise and fall and a new king is born
Why do our children's dreams lie forlorn?

Look Closely

Look closely
You will see
A grandmother selling *buai*[39] to make ends meet
Carrying the world on her shoulders
Why chase her to her death?
Do you see her?

Look closely
You will see
A boy who didn't complete his education
He steals a few kinas to survive
Why do you beat him up?
Do you see him?

Look closely
You will see
A young lady from a broken family
She frequents the clubs for clients
To put food on the table
Why do you call her names?
Do you see her?

Look closely
You will see
A father surviving on a shoe-string budget
Living on the wings of a prayer
Why are we so selfish?
Do you see him?

---

[39] Buai: Betel nut

Look closely
You will see
Public servants working their asses off
While clowns in the *Haus Tambaran*[40]
Play frolicking power games
Why is there so much corruption?
Do you see us?

Look closely
Look harder
Look deeper
You just might see
The world from our eyes.

---

[40] Haus Tambaran: Parliament House

A LOVE POEM

1.
I'm your 'twilight's child'
In the blue gardens of dawn
When the soul is quiet
I'll whisper to you the secrets of morning.
2.
I'm your 'pearl in the mist'
When you're lost in the journey of life
And you think you're blown away
Like a petal in the wind
I'll show you the gates of paradise.
3.
I'm your 'white, hot angel'
When the mountains too high to climb
And you can't go another mile alone
I'll help you carry on.
4.
I'm your 'Romeo'
With the passage of cloudy days
When you're listening to the drumming rain
Trickle, trickle, trickle
I'll shelter you from the rain.
5.
I'm your 'golden shooting star'
In the darkest hour of night
When shadows shrink and rise
And you're too blind to find your way home
I'll rescue you from the storm.
6.
I'm your 'prince charming'
When the lines of tension dig themselves
Deeper and deeper into your face
Like the print of ugly memories
And there's no one to comfort you
I'll be your strength, I'll keep you warm.

7.
I'm your 'apple in the eye'
When you feel immobilized
And there's nothing to hold onto
I'll give you hope.
8.
I'm your 'hidden jewel'
Of tarnished gold and all that glitters
In the garden of fallen hearts
I'll make your dreams come true.
9.
I'm your 'doctor of love'
When the ties of love seem to be unwinding
And the ribbons of your heart
Are deeply lacerated;

I'll sing to you a melody —
A love song
To heal your crippled heart.

The World around Us

Eyeless Kin

Mansions you have my uncles
Money you have my brothers
Shops you own my cousins
In your fancy cars you whizz
Past me without stopping
To say hello.

I wonder if you have eyes
To see that the blood in you
And the one that runs in me
Are but the same
But it's only water now
Each man for his own
A world of eyeless kin.

In the hot *mosbi*[41] sun
Waiting to catch a bus
In my little basket
I carry my dreams.

Winds don't always blow
In the same direction
And one glorious day
I will whizz past you
Like a stranger too.

---

[41] Mosbi: Port Moresby

INDEPENDENCE DAY

Wind whips unsteady fingers of rain
On a sun-stricken holiday
And the air is filled with joy
Colourful flags adorned the sky
Sons and daughters of this land
Sing the national anthem
Dance to the beat of the *kundu*[42]
Papua New Guinean dream
Redeemed by political rhetoric   ·
Everywhere a sense of belonging
To a place in which I don't belong
Until the rain and I met
In recognition and open fingers
It's raining heavily in my soul
My pocket, empty and broke
Thought I'd make a fortune
But I'd never been so empty.

---

[42] Kundu: Traditional drum

SP LAGER

At the Cosmopolitan
I greedily gulp twelve bottles of SP
The alcohol flows though my veins
Exploding in my head
Like a silver Roman candle
I see a thousand stars
It thumps my chest
And flows down my arms
And through the rest of my body
Like liquid gold.
I feel myself floating above the clouds
It feels so good
I laugh and groan.

Its hangover;
Cruel fate over!
Everything over!

SATURDAY NIGHT

Last Saturday night
I tried to drown all my worries
Watched my youthful twenty five years
Floating in a glass of cock-tail
Spent my night out partying
At the grooviest places in town
Dancing with those pretty girls at the club
This cock-tail has the flavour
To ease all my worries
A thousand stars twinkle before my eyes
Depression is a word only whispered.

Sunday morning
Finds me hidden beneath my covers
Still studying my problems
Some stupid bitch blaming me
As the father of her child
She deserved that one night stand
Should have used a condom
To avoid this silly pregnancy headache.

I'm here in my room
Surrounded with words
Disoriented, disconcerted
My head spins!

FALSE MESSIAH (POLITICIAN)

Out of his sugar-coated mouth
Came words of gold
And promises of development.
Praise the Lord for such a servant!

We thought he was the messiah
Sent from the *Haus Tambaran*[43]
To heal our *moni sicknesses*[44]
And give us our daily bread
Oh Hallelujah!

We voted him
And made him king
Time passed
One year, two years
He never returned.

Tough luck for us
'Oh Father, hallowed by thy name
Please hear our cries
And send your messiah back to us
Amen'.

Alas, there's no answers
Only prayers.

---

[43] Haus Tambaran: Parliament House
[44] Moni sicknesses: Financial woes

CANDIDATES

Election came once again
Candidates came
Different parties
Different posters
Different bribes
Different leaders
Different colours
Different promises.

Pink promises
Green promises
Yellow promises
Making us colour blind
We are disillusioned
By power-hungry candidates
Who forget all their promises
When they get to Waigani.

A Circus

Haus Tambaran[45] is a circus
Full of immature monkeys
Calling each other names
Playing number games.

The king is a chimpanzee
He feeds all the monkeys
With golden bananas
And they grow pot bellies.

We the people suffer
And gossip silently
Not our monkeys!
Not our circus!

---

[45] Haus Tambaran: Parliament House

WHEN I AM THE PRIME MINISTER

Another lifeless day
The leaves are brown
My mind is cloudy
Waiting for the bus at Waigani
Around me
All the noise of the world
Buai[46] sellers, noisy bus crews
All struggling to earn some money
For their next meal.

Where do all our taxes go?
Emotions rising
Anger peaking
All so confusing
Politics
Seriously?
This must be a big joke
Poly-many, many wives
Poly-steal, corrupt deals
Poly-tricks, liars
Blood sucking parasites
Truth.

It's getting late
We rush like sardines
To hitch a ride on the last buses
'Bus fare, bus fare, *wasa*[47] bus fare!'
Bus crew cuts into my reverie
I hand him over a kina
'Keep the change'
He smiled.

---

[46] Buai: Betel nut
[47] Wasa: One kina

Problems of yesterday gone
Trees will look a little greener
And people will smile
When I am the Prime Minister.

Two-Faced Saints

You pray every Monday morning
For divine guidance and blessing
But I see two-faced saints
Self-interest and affluence
Nepotism and religion-ism
Are you praying to the right God?

What are our core values again?
Saw it somewhere in our policies
Maybe I should just keep quiet
Get more loans from Moni-Plus
Watch my net pay further minus
'Til the next increment to enjoy a beer
In this world of unequal opportunities.

Economic crises?
No worries!
It's in our annual work plan
Just send a relative to Japan
To attend APEC meetings
Internet of Things
And concept papers
Will benefit rural farmers
What are our priorities again?

Two-faced saints
Bible in one pocket
The other, a thick wallet
My thoughts are tormented
Forgive me if I have sinned
I whisper a silent prayer
I beg Jesus for a quiet life.

TAX EVERYTHING

Tax my house
Tax my cigarettes
Tax my drinks
Tax my rice and tinned fish
Tax my superannuation
Tax my savings and pay
 I am working for peanuts anyway!

Tax my water
Tax my play box
Tax my electricity
Tax my plane ticket
Tax my vehicle
Tax my petrol and gas
Find other ways to tax my ass!

Tax my clothes
Tax my medicines
Tax my pig
Tax my dog
Tax my wife
Tax everything I have!

Tax my coffin
Tax my headstone
Tax my grave
Even the soil in which I am buried.

And when I am gone
My inheritance remains
With the Public Curator
To be taxed some more!

FATHERLESS CHILD

His dad is a Chinese man
Who owned several shops
A love child that came by chance
Illegitimate as they say
By-product of unplanned romance
One-too-many drinks and a quick lay.

Tequilas kept coming
Courtesy of the Chinese
Boozed up lady
One night stand she'd soon forget
Baby's daddy gone
After his desires were met.

Forgotten Christmas cards
No birthday cakes
Life shows no mercy.

Forgotten dreams
Happiness is just a dream
For a fatherless child.

MY ROOM MATE

The rat is an unlawful tenant
It lives on unscrupulous profit
Earned from dirty schemes
Yet pays no rental for his accommodation.

He chews my clothes
Eats up my food
Even wants to bite my toes
But still insists on being my roommate.

FIREWORKS

Pinwheels whirling around
Spitting sparks upon the ground
Rockets shoot up high
And blossom in the night sky
Blue and yellow, green and red flowers
Falling onto my head
Like a glittering crown.

VISITOR

A strange little green frog
Came
                    Hop up the stairs
          Hop
     Hop
He looked at the door, he looked at the mat
He looked at this and he looked at that
He looked at me
And went hop
                    Hop
                         Hop down the stairs again.

JACKSONS AIRPORT

At the Jacksons airport
I see metallic eagles
Taking off the runway
They glide into the air
Soaring higher and higher
Into the warm sky
Until they're gone
Through the clouds
That looks like floating icebergs.

THE SEA

The sea is my girlfriend
She cheers me up when I'm gloomy
And agrees with whatever I say
When happy, she rushes back and forth
With quick little splashes
Of beautiful, blue colour
When angry, she is all choppy
With white dogs looking very fierce
On warm days I lie on her sand
Of pure white silk and dream.

Port Moresby

Port Moresby stretched out before me
Resplendent, glorious, magical
And gleaming in the tropical sun.

But my heart weeps for this jungle
Of glass and steel skeletons;
A city of cock-tail parties,
Home-brew for all the street boys
And *spak-brus*[48] for the drug-bodies.

When the sun comes sailing down
I see the blue van patrolling around
And out in the city's streets
A silhouetted figure is asking
For one kina.

---

[48] Spak brus: Marijuana

Short Verse & Prose

Haiku, Quatrain, Clerihew, Quinzaine, Limerick, Tanka, Sijo, Cinquain & Gogyohka

EMPIRE

A small ant searching
Among the dry, yellow leaves
Building an empire.

SELFIE

Blue sky, green trees - smile
Twisted bodies, fish lips pursed
Taking a selfie!

COMPLICATED

Two bastard children
And two failed relationships
It's complicated!

SINGLE LIFE

An empty bottle
Washed upon a lonely shore
Single life is no fun.

HOPE

Pearly kernels sprout
Golden sunflower blossoms
Hope is like a seed.

LOVELY DAISY

Lovely daisy blooms
A flower never competes
To look beautiful.

SMALL FISH

Small fish in the pond
No ripples are never felt
Across the ocean.

LOVE FALSIFIED

A ray of sunshine
Disappeared in the rain
A love falsified.

SECRETS

A soft white ripple
Placidly flowing river
So many secrets.

WARRIOR

Fierce warrior
Conquering endless battles
A woman endures.

GENDER CONFUSION

Heavy make-up done
Ladies clothing plus a wig
Turn him into her.

CROCODILE TEARS

I watch your tears fall
And think of a crocodile
Knowing it's a lie.

SHOWER GEL

Mini heart attack
Sweet fragrance of shower gel
When you walked past me.

TWO FACED

She carries sunshine
And darkness equally well
Angel and demon.

TUNA SEASON

Yellow rosewood leaves
Turn to burnished brown and fall
Season for tuna.

YAM HARVEST SEASON

July monsoon winds
Bringing rain and thunderstorms
Yam harvest season.

BAD SPIRITS

On a moonless night
Fireflies emitting light
Warn of bad spirits.

GOLDEN HAIR

Long golden hair flows
Down her back to her slim waist
Girl from the islands.

WHITEMAN IN BLACK SKIN

Flaunt a fancy accent
On your return from Aussie
Whiteman in black skin.

SUNDI WANAKU

Cold, misty morning
Beauty in desolation
Sundi wanaku[49].

---

[49] Sundi wanaku: Young lady from Enga

COSMETICS

Face painted with clay
Like an Asaro mud man
Too much cosmetics.

MY FLAG

Red, black and yellow
Fly high beautiful *kumul*[50]
My flag, my country.

AIGIR

Coconut creamed food
Greens with chicken and spices
Sweet Tolai *aigir*[51].

CHILDHOOD MEMORIES

Silver moon rising
Chasing crabs along the sand
Childhood memories.

---

[50] Kumul: Bird of Paradise
[51] Aigir: Traditional Tolai style of cooking

BROWN SKINNED GIRL

Brown skinned girl
Like chocolate
Gifted, articulate
You make my heart twirl.

RED SUNSET

The horizon turned red
Like blood on high
When darkness pierced
The evening sky.

O'NAMAH

First we applauded O'Namah
Thought they'd be like Obama
When they displaced Somare
Goodbye laissez-faire!

FAKE HAIR

Over-braided highlander
Where's the natural hair?
Why so fake?

WITCH

Light skinned lady from Milne Bay
Do you fly at night?
Should I run?

BROTHER FROM THE HIGHLANDS

My brother from the highlands
Have you seen a shark?
Can you swim?

BROTHER FROM THE COASTLANDS

My brother from the coastlands
Do you have many pigs?
Why one wife?

COSMOPOLITAN CAGE DANCER

In the cage, she dances with grace
A mischievous smile upon her face
Semi-naked and bare
But she doesn't care
To her family, she's a disgrace!

CITY LOOP TAXI

The taxis are owned by Malaysians
The tucker boxes are run by Asians
We are now like the beggars
Paid with a few hamburgers
Enough of this nonsense, we're Christians!

SHOOTING STAR

Watch the moon tonight
You'll see me dancing gaily
With my new lover
My aura embracing her
A shooting star is her solace.

POLITICS OF GREED

A forbidden tree
Nourishes on corruption
Abode of monkeys
Infecting public servants
With its poisonous apples.

MIDNIGHT SUN

To the midnight sun
I have made a small request
A frangipani
Crafted in the starless sky
From my silent dew dropped words.

SILENT LOVE

Her love can only be heard
Like silent footsteps
Within her heartbeat
Seen in her eyes
Tasted on her lips.

MEMORIES

Memories
Bitter, Sweet
Everlasting, enduring, unfading
I cherish those moments
Together.

HEARTACHE

Heart
Delicate, crushed
Shattering, breaking, bleeding
You cut me deep
Ache.

CHASING RAINBOWS

Never be/ afraid to chase/
    your colorful/ rainbow where ever
It may lead/ though most of us/
    shall never find/ the rainbows end
Those who do/ know it's where heaven/
    has kissed the earth/ and lingered.

A NEW DAWN

Close your eyes/ take a deep breath/
    let the waves take/ all your worries
Out to sea/ let the warmth/
    of the sun stir/ those embers left
To smolder/ and ignite the flames/
    like a new day/ a new dawn.

TO A YOUNG LADY

Young lady/ listen to me/
    do not marry/ that old white man
He is old/ enough to be/
    your grandfather/ aren't you shy?
I know/ money is scarce but/
    don't clip your wings/you can soar high.

www.ingramcontent.com/pod-product-compliance
Lightning Source LLC
Chambersburg PA
CBHW052130090426
42741CB00009B/2030

9789980899859